T0198561

Winter Faith

Neal Thompson

AuthorHouse™
1663 Liberty Drive
Bloomington, IN 47403
www.authorhouse.com
Phone: 1 (800) 839-8640

Because of the dynamic nature of the Internet, any web addresses or links contained in this book may have changed since publication and may no longer be valid. The views expressed in this work are solely those of the author and do not necessarily reflect the views of the publisher, and the publisher hereby disclaims any responsibility for them.

Any people depicted in stock imagery provided by Getty Images are models, and such images are being used for illustrative purposes only.
Certain stock imagery © Getty Images.

This book is printed on acid-free paper.

Scripture quotations marked NIV are taken from the Holy Bible, New International Version®. NIV®. Copyright © 1973, 1978, 1984 by International Bible Society. Used by permission of Zondervan. All rights reserved. [Biblica]

ISBN: 978-1-7283-4541-3 (sc)
ISBN: 978-1-7283-4540-6 (e)

Library of Congress Control Number: 2020901792

Print information available on the last page.

Published by AuthorHouse 02/25/2020

authorHOUSE®

For My Wife

Who makes everything I write possible

Acknowledgments

Boundary Community Hospital

Boundary County Sheriffs Office and Prosecutors Office

Montana State Hospital

Bonners Ferry Museum

Troy Police Department, Troy Montana

Disability Right's, Helena Montana

Anaconda Montana Sheriffs Department

Imagines obtained from www.unsplash.com

Special Thanks To:

Everyone that helped with <u>Crazy Loves Crazy.</u>

Levi Falck: Who stuck with the story from the beginning to the end. It wasn't days of discussion and research, it was fifteen years. If your house was on fire, do you think God would send a librarian? God chooses men with the skills to complete the tasks. If someone you loved was taken/ abducted, I hope God sends Levi.

3mm Investigations
Faith Foundation
Nathan Gomez
Andy Falck
Big Levi Faulkner
Gina Beck L.C.S.W
Steve Brown
Tina Puckette
Jon Erikson jr
David West
Jay Gross

and of course my publisher:
   Author House

Winter Faith

By Neal Thompson

Romans 12:21

Do not be overcome by evil, but overcome evil with good.

Winter Time

A time of the year when the air is cold, bones feel old and God keeps the beer cold.

A time to climb, a time to fall

A time to stand on top of the mountain and remember them all forgetting the fall

because it's time to climb it's winter time!

Tracks in the snow

It is all tracks in the snow that melt and leave in the spring
Enjoying the colors and fresh air,
You think of those tracks and where they went
Some went places where nobody else could follow,
Through the clouds, to the top of the mountain
You look back down in amazement that you made it, and smile
Then you remember you are the only one there,
And start thinking of all the friends that couldn't ride with you.
I still listen for their sled.

December 2010

Nothing

It has been over a year since we held each other
Two months since Mary was free.
What I feel, I would not wish on anybody

Her and I have so much love, it has become destructive.
Being in the same house is now terrifying.
I tried so hard for so many years
To remember and put the pieces in place.

Now it is a flood;
Every moment,
Her smell,
Her touch.
Things we said, I could not remember
All the emotions I tried to lock up
Are all out of twelve years of terror.

January 2016

Flippen The Switch

This happens to an elite group of men and women,
For us the switch is on the handlebar.
flippen the switch ceases life as we see it
We go to places most people can't.

A place high above everything,
Where some stay,
Where some get out.

Sometimes only with help, do we make it back
People who don't understand, think we are crazy
Others try and crash
We have learned to fall, so we can climb higher
We pick places out of the snow,
To put it back together again.

I lay awake waiting for dawn to break
Feeling the ache in my heart.

Remembering the start,
Remembering the day we had to part.

Every part of my soul is withing you back.

Homee, I'm the Love:
You see me everyday in Alicia and little kids.
Remember who you are,
Who made you.

Remember who I am.
The love is in your homee,
The foundation is you heart.

Faith Ann Swinney

November 2012

Where Is God?

He is everywhere,
with a promise of love everlasting.
I thought I knew God and could always feel him,
but when things went wrong,
I chose my own devices, instead of having
Faith!

Until God sent and angel.
She did not stay long,
just twelve days.
She tested my faith like never before.

I wanted her to stay longer,
but God had other plans.
The love I learned from her outweighed,
the pain of losing her.
That love kept me alive.

Always having faith,
God would bring us back together again and
he did for another short time.
That's when I learned,
we had never been apart and never will be.

In just a short time:
She altered the path of so many lives
Forever.
It has taken a lot of tears and sleepness nights
to understand Faith.
She will hold my heart and soul for eternity and I hers.

Not everyone has an angel for a wife.
March 2013

Easter Sunday

Love got me in
Love will get me out

Faith

The Tree In Me

A tree cannot pee
or bend at the knee, but
you will see.
The tree is where God wanted it to be,
it cannot flee
God gave it plenty.

It does not worry about food or water
Nor can it run from fire.
It was made to bend in the fiercest winds
and stand back up again.

But what about you and me,
are we a tree?
I am Homee

I am your light
I am your love
I am your Faith

Share our love
Share what I gave you.

Faith

August 2013

I am a poet
and didn't know it.
instead of a fighter.
A lover
that wont run for cover

Prologue…
Crazy Loves Crazy
Knocking on the Gates of Hell

It's been six years, how did I get here? How did this happen? Driving the camouflage Chevy through the high mountain desert of Montana. The sun is just starting to rise and the snow finally stopped, it is twenty degrees. I must be getting close, been on the road for seven hours. Stopping at a little Mom N Pops gas station and getting the fifth mug of coffee and some Copenhagen, the clerk asked me "is that everything?"

Well actually, "I am trying to find the State Hospital."

"Oh! You mean Warm Spring's; you passed the turn a few miles back."

"Warm Springs?"

"Yeah, that's what they call it."

"Okay, Thanks. Have a good day."

"You too."

Back on the road, I see the sign eight miles to Warm Springs. My mind is racing, my heart is pounding. Is it really her, alive this whole time?

Neal is fifty-two now, living in a new cabin in the mountains of north Idaho. Huggy and Bees had puppies. Neal loves his poms and fly-fishing. He still loves Mary who now resides at Warm Spring's. Years later Neal and Levi started their own investigation company to find out what happened to Mary. The results were shocking to say the least.

Printed in the United States
By Bookmasters